Disclaimers

*The quotes in this book, outside of Scripture, are intended to inspire and encourage readers. It is important to note that the inclusion of these quotes does not imply any endorsement of any particular individual's beliefs or lifestyles, either past, present, or future. The author of this book does not condone any views or actions that may be associated with the individuals quoted.

*The stories included in this book are based on actual events and people. However, the names and other identifying details have been changed to protect the privacy and anonymity of those involved.

BOOK 1

DESTINED  TO SHINE

SECURING YOUR TRUE IDENTITY

MARY CHALHOUB

KINGDOM ROAR

Book 1
Securing Your True Identity

© 2024 Mary Chalhoub

For more information, visit: www.marychalhoub.com

Print – 979-8-9882041-0-7
eBook – 979-8-9882041-1-4

Scriptures marked ESV are taken from THE HOLY BIBLE, ENGLISH STANDARD VERSION (ESV): Scriptures taken from THE HOLY BIBLE, ENGLISH STANDARD VERSION ® Copyright© 2001 by Crossway, a publishing ministry of Good News Publishers.
Used by permission.

Scriptures marked GW are taken from the GOD'S WORD (GW): Scripture taken from GOD'S WORD® copyright© 1995 by God's Word to the Nations. All rights reserved.

Scriptures marked KJV are taken from the KING JAMES VERSION (KJV): KING JAMES VERSION, public domain.

Scriptures marked NAS are taken from the NEW AMERICAN STANDARD (NAS): Scripture taken from the NEW AMERICAN STANDARD BIBLE®, copyright© 1960, 1962, 1963, 1968, 1971,

Dedication

To God, my Father and Creator, who rescued me from darkness and led me to the light. I pray that through the power of the Holy Spirit, the words in this book bring glory and honor to the name of Your Son, Jesus, my Lord and Savior, the One whom I love.

Endorsements

prophetic edge, but also her writing. It's to the point, practical and worth your time to read. I believe this series will take your walk with God to another level which is a need I hear of all the time in many circles. It would behoove you to add *Destined to Shine: Securing Your True Identity* to your literary library.

-John Veal, Author of *Destroying Demonic Tactics: 8 Supernatural Strategies to Defeat Satan's Newest Schemes*

* * * * *

Destined to Shine: Securing Your True Identity is a life-empowering, transformative resource for unlocking the heart of the *true you*. Mary Chalhoub gives clear and detailed understanding of how the human heart is deeply affected by relationships, trauma, and the connection with its Maker, Father God. The immense amount of vulnerability, insight, and wisdom keys that she shares will cause the deadest of hearts to come alive and step into a new, purposeful life - a life each one of us were made to live and enjoy.

-Robyn F. Vincent, Author of *The Rise of the Overcomer*

* * * * *

I was drawn in from the very beginning of the first chapter. Mary Chalhoub does a wonderful job of connecting us to the vital nature of the subject from the start. Having written about identity myself, I could truly relate to the issue of arrested development and the lack of self-worth that keep us from receiving the love of the Father. Recognizing that we are in a spiritual battle—more than a physical one—helps us to turn our attention to the One who is able to heal us. Through *Destined to Shine: Securing Your True Identity*, Mary exposes, explains, and equips us on this journey to recovering who we are in Christ.

-James Vincent, Author, Minister, and Recording Artist

* * * * *

Mary Chalhoub captures the true heart and mind of the father's love in this book, *Destined to Shine: Securing Your True Identity*. It is packed with keys to deliverance, restoration, and healing. I have not experienced the gentleness of God's love in writing as I have in this book. Mary's life and pursuit to see others free from the bondages that plague our true purpose in life can be felt with conviction and forgiveness in this amazing book series. I am confronted deeply with love, liberty, and freedom to be me.

-Kathryn Summers, Author of
The Dynamics of Prophetic Worship

The Destined to S.H.I.N.E. Series

Do you sense God is calling you to something greater than yourself? If so, now is the time to answer His call. Your destiny can't wait. Whether you have a book to write, a business to launch, or a dream to fulfill, your decision will impact your own life and the lives of those around you, leaving a lasting legacy that will continue to inspire generations to come. Your purpose can be the catalyst for someone else's victory. They need you to rise and shine!

This series was born from a vision God gave me many years ago. Although I initially hesitated, God repeatedly confirmed that this was His assignment for me. After eight years of hard work and pushing through adversity, finally, the first book was published. While you can read each book independently, I recommend reading them chronologically to get the most out of the series.

The *Destined to S.H.I.N.E.* series is a scripturally based, interactive study designed to help you live your God-given dreams with joy, confidence, and purpose. The series takes you on a journey that begins by focusing on the inner workings of the soul and guides you toward boldly fulfilling the call of God on your life.

Book One, *Securing Your True Identity*, explores the transformative power in breaking free from limiting beliefs and embracing God's limitless love. You will learn how to conquer the inner battles of the mind and align with the mind of Christ, enabling you to recognize your inherent worth and walk fearlessly in your true identity.

Book Two, *Healing Your Heart*, leads you into freedom and wholeness through the discipline of fasting and the essential keys to forgiveness that aid in unlocking emotional and physical healing. Additionally, you will gain valuable insight into establishing healthy boundaries and cultivating thriving relationships.

Book Three, *Impacting Your World*, helps you discover your unique mix of gifts, talents, and abilities and explains how to utilize them to bless others and fulfill your purpose. Moreover, you will understand how to live by powerful kingdom principles and effectively use your voice to make a lasting impact in your sphere of influence.

Book Four, *Navigating Your Dreams*, supports you in realizing your God-given dreams by equipping you with the skills to write out a clear vision and take actionable steps toward achieving your goals. You will also develop the ability to overcome obstacles and persevere during challenging times.

Book Five, *Experiencing God's Promises*, emphasizes the importance of surrendering everything to God and adopting a heavenly perspective that empowers you to walk in supernatural faith through the Holy Spirit. Aligned with God's purposes, you will ultimately experience His promises and shine with His glory!

A Note from the Author

I find great joy in partnering with God to help others experience life-changing transformations and break-throughs. Throughout this series, I'll share many of these incredible stories and testimonies, including my own experiences. I sincerely hope that the words in these books will empower you to fulfill your unique calling, bringing glory to God. Supporting you on your journey to live the authentic, victorious life God intended for you is both an honor and a privilege. And I look forward to hearing your personal testimonies as you read through the series.

This journey is much like that of a diamond. In Romans 8:37, Paul declares that despite life's challenges, you are not merely a conqueror but more than that. Interestingly, the word diamond derives from the Greek word *adámas*, which means "unconquerable.[i]" Similar to how a diamond is formed under pressure, God will use the trials, disappointments, and losses to strengthen, form, and fashion you for a life of success.

Jesus has a brilliant future planned for you, and He won't waste anything you've ever been through. It's time to say "yes" to His call.

You are Destined to SHINE!

Mary Chalhoub

Contents

CHAPTER 1

Experiencing the Power of Love

"The love of God is not a doctrine,
but an experience."
~William Barclay

A WAR OVER MY LIFE

At the age of twenty-five, I found myself overwhelmed by relentless pain and disappointment. One night, at my breaking point, I cried out to God in deep despair, "Take me, take my life! I can't go on like this!" Exhausted from countless sleepless nights, I collapsed onto my bed, and then something extraordinary happened. Gradually, I felt myself rising, and as I glanced around the room, I realized that I was floating in midair.

Looking back at my bed, I saw my body still lying there. Overwhelmed with confusion, I couldn't help but wonder, "Is this even possible? Am I in the Twilight Zone?"

As I hovered in this surreal moment, the walls of my room began to fade, and I found myself standing in a realm of utter darkness on my left and blinding light to my right. Then, a sudden fear gripped me as a deep, angry voice from the darkness growled, "She's mine!"

But then, a comforting presence wrapped around me like a warm blanket. A loving yet firm voice emerged from the radiant light, declaring, "No! She is my beloved daughter, and you will never have her!"

Instantly, I felt the stomach-dropping sensation of a free fall, as if plummeting down a roller coaster at full speed, landing abruptly but softly. Gasping in disbelief, I became aware that I was back in my body, lying on my bed. From that day onward, life would never be the same.

I couldn't make sense of what had just transpired, but one thing became unmistakably clear—there was a war over my life, a battle between darkness and light. In that very moment, Satan and God became undeniably real to me, and I understood that both sought to claim my soul.

After that encounter, the days that followed opened a floodgate of memories and revelations. It was as though something within me had unlocked, exposing how I had always believed I was not pretty enough, talented enough, simply not good enough. This realization led me to question why accepting and loving myself the way God made me was so challenging.

Was it because I had found out that I was an unplanned child, or because I had been bullied in middle school, or perhaps because I had doubted my parents' love for me? These experiences might have contributed to my agreement with the voice of self-hatred. However, what mattered most was God heard my desperate cry for help. That pivotal moment ignited my faith and led me on a journey of healing and deliverance.

The Holy Spirit took on a mentoring role in my life, distinctly different from what my traditional Christian background had taught me. As my desire to know God deepened, so did my experience of His love, leading to a profound transformation within me. Through this journey of discovering my true identity, I learned to accept and love myself the way God does, which enabled me to extend that same love to others.

THE MAIN GOAL

Scripture makes it clear that our primary purpose in life is to love, which is also the reason for our existence. We are created not only to experience love but also to share it with others. However, to give love, we must first have it within us. While everyone's understanding of love can differ, we should look to God's Word for guidance. A fundamental truth from 1 John 4:8 tells us that if we do not have love, we do not truly know God, for God is love.

Additionally, 1 Corinthians 13:4-7 (NIV) describes the characteristics of love, stating: "Love is patient, love is kind. It does not envy, it does not boast, it is not proud. It does not dishonor others, it is not self-seeking, it is not easily angered, it keeps no record of wrongs. Love does not delight in evil but rejoices with the truth. It always protects, always trusts, always hopes, always perseveres."

While we are encouraged to share love with others, it is equally important to extend that same love to ourselves. Take a moment to contemplate the characteristics of love, and ask yourself: Do I embody patience and kindness toward myself, or do I hold onto anger and keep records of my mistakes?

In my own journey, I found it difficult to love myself and others, mainly due to past negative experiences that left me feeling unworthy of love. It wasn't until I discovered God's love and committed to a personal relationship with Jesus that I started to recognize my worth and true identity in Him. Through years of mentoring and ministering to others, I've come to realize that this internal struggle is quite common.

WHAT SELF-LOVE IS

Understanding self-love can be challenging for some people. This difficulty often stems from the misconception that self-love equates to idolatry or self-worship. However, this interpretation misunderstands the true nature of love. While it's true that we should not worship ourselves, practicing self-love is essential.

According to Webster's dictionary, worship is the act of honoring or revering someone as a divine being or showing them extravagant respect or devotion. This concept is distinct from self-love. Our human nature often leans toward self-worship, an excessive and inappropriate focus on ourselves that can elevate us to a divine status. In contrast, practicing self-love requires discipline and understanding.

Another common misbelief is that self-love is simply about pursuing personal happiness. It's important to clarify that seeking happiness is not wrong in itself; however, relying solely on external sources for happiness, apart from God, can lead to self-centeredness.

True self-love is a far cry from arrogance, conceit, or a belief in superiority over others. It involves seeing ourselves through the lens of God's perspective; this means acknowledging that we are fearfully and wonderfully created by God without any mistakes in His design. Self-love is about coming to terms with both the aspects of ourselves we cannot change and the unique qualities, gifts, and talents God has given us. It means fully accepting who we are and cultivating a healthy regard for ourselves, knowing that we are valued as beloved children of God.

FOLLOWING JESUS' EXAMPLE

While on earth, Jesus was deeply aware of His worth and led a life filled with purpose. Empowered by love, He devoted Himself to touching the lives of others through His teachings and acts of service. The love that Jesus demonstrated continues to make an impact even today. By laying down His life, His sacrifice not only brought us life but also purpose.

The transformative love of God reshapes our hearts, making it possible for us to love others genuinely. This truth is captured in 1 John 4:19, "We love because He first loved us." Receiving this primary love is vital for developing a healthy sense of self-love and acceptance, which allows us to extend this love to others. The sacrificial act of Jesus lays the groundwork for our understanding of personal worth and value, affirming that we are precious because Jesus paid the ultimate price for us.

While you and I are not Jesus, we are called to follow His example. He gave us two of the greatest commandments for us to live by, as recorded in Matthew 22:37-39 (NLT), "Jesus replied, 'You must love the Lord your God with all your heart, all your soul, and all your mind.' This is the first and greatest commandment. A second is equally important: 'Love your neighbor as yourself.'"

Both commandments highlight the importance of self-love. The first suggests that we cannot wholeheartedly love God if we despise His creation, including ourselves. Loving God fully involves loving and accepting ourselves as part of His creation. The second indicates that the love we show our neighbors reflects the love that we have for ourselves. Essentially, the way we treat others often mirrors how we view and treat ourselves.

Living out these commandments is essential for advancing the kingdom of heaven, although it comes with challenges. Matthew 12:25 (ESV) warns, "no house divided against itself will stand," highlighting the importance of internal harmony. Satan understands the power of walking in these two commandments and will attempt to prevent us from this revelation.

THE INTERNAL CONFLICT

The adversary seeks to divide us internally by sowing seeds of self-doubt, inadequacy, and a sense of unworthiness. He skillfully manipulates our thoughts and emotions, leading to feelings of insecurity. Often, he uses tactics like drawing unfavorable comparisons with others or bringing up past failures to intensify self-criticism.

If these tactics are successful, they can lead to us rejecting parts or even all of ourselves. This rejection can then lead to self-hatred, further deepening the internal divide. Such inner turmoil makes it difficult to achieve peace and wholeness. To effectively deal with this problem, it's crucial to identify and confront the real enemy.

Ephesians 6:12 (NAS) reminds us, "For our struggle is not against flesh and blood, but against the rulers, against the powers, against the world forces of this darkness, against the spiritual forces of wickedness in the heavenly places."

This scripture serves as a powerful reminder: our struggle isn't against ourselves or anyone else but rather a battle against Satan and the forces of darkness. Therefore, we must end the inner conflict by shifting our focus from self-criticism to self-acceptance. In doing so, we can focus on what matters most and live a more purposeful life.

God doesn't merely desire us to know about Him; He yearns for a personal relationship with each of us through Jesus. While our experiences with God may vary, His love for us remains consistent. If you harbor doubts or reservations about His love for you, I encourage you to seek Him for a personal revelation.

Realizing the depth of God's love for you is key to uncovering your true identity. This love does more than affirm; it transforms you, molding your character and potential. Remember, your existence itself is a testament to His love. You are not just a creation; you are born out of love, meant to embody and share this love, and through this love, you are destined to make a meaningful difference in the world.

ACTIVATIONS

Take your time to journal your answers to the following questions. Be honest with your feelings.

1. Review the description of love in 1 Corinthians 13:4-7 and reflect on whether you apply these characteristics of love to yourself. Record your thoughts. Then, consider how embodying the love described in this passage might affect your interactions and behavior toward others.

2. Read through Psalm 139, line by line. What specific verses or insights speak to you about God's intentional design and His complete understanding of you? Use this as a basis for your prayer, inviting Him to make His love known to you through Jesus. Trust, wait, and expect Him to demonstrate His love, which may come in the most unexpected ways.

CHAPTER 2

Receiving the Love of the Father

"God loves each of us as if there were only one of us."
~Saint Augustine of Hippo

LOOKING FOR AFFECTION

My father expressed his love in the way he knew how. He was the stable provider for our family, a source of wise counsel, and the one whose dry sense of humor could effortlessly bring smiles to everyone's faces. Yet, throughout my childhood, the words "I love you" remained unspoken, and the warmth of his embrace was something I rarely recalled. This lack of affection didn't mean his love was absent; instead, he was a man shaped by his own upbringing, one where such emotional expressions were foreign.

During my younger years, my dad's job frequently took him overseas, resulting in extended periods without his presence at home. Each return home was bittersweet, marked by mixed emotions where joy was often overshadowed by conflicts. His parenting style, deeply rooted in the traditions of his Egyptian heritage, frequently clashed with my growing personal values. I felt as though my voice was unheard and often unfavorably compared to that of others. As time passed, I found myself withdrawing, building emotional walls, yet silently longing for his acceptance.

In high school, I was the quiet girl who had never had a boyfriend and wasn't into dating. This changed during my senior year when I attended a party at my friend's house, where I met a guy who initially didn't spark my interest. However, over time, his persistent pursuit began to fill a deep void within me, one that yearned for attention and affection.

This relationship, as it turned out, led to heartbreak. And not long after its end, I found myself in a similar relationship with a different guy. We dreamed of a future together and even planned for marriage, but betrayal struck just a week before our engagement announcement.

My world turned upside down, and I spiraled into a deep depression. Not wanting to experience that kind of pain again, I vowed not to enter another serious relationship until I was absolutely certain, with God's confirmation, that I had found the man He intended for me to marry.

FOLLOWING GOD'S PLANS

After completing my pharmacy degree from the University of Houston and starting my career as a pharmacist, I felt a subtle yet profound stirring in my heart. It was as if God was leading me toward a different path beyond my current profession. I sensed there was more that God had planned for me.

In my search for spiritual growth, a friend invited me to a home church led by pastors fresh from their experience at Toronto Airport Christian Fellowship (TACF), known for experiencing a spiritual phenomenon called the Toronto Blessing. With passion, they spoke about the revival they had witnessed—a mighty outpouring of the Father's love that had profoundly touched and healed them. Their testimonies resonated with me, igniting a longing to experience this revival for myself.

Shortly after becoming a member of this church, they organized a group trip to attend a conference at TACF.

Without hesitation, I joined them. Weeks later, we embarked on our journey there, and as soon as I stepped through the church doors, God's tangible, weighty presence overwhelmed me. It was an experience like no other I had ever known.

While making my way through the vast sanctuary, I was struck by the sheer number of people visibly touched by God. Laughter, tears, and dancing filled the room. It was evident that there was a powerful anointing for breaking chains in that atmosphere of the Father's love.

Throughout the conference, I had the privilege of meeting people who had traveled from every corner of the world to experience His presence. By the final session, I, too, was deeply touched by the Father's heart. Carrying this profound revelation home with me, I had a strong sense that my journey there was only the beginning, and that it would not be my last.

On my way out, a table with information about their school of ministry caught my attention. Compelled by a deep sense of purpose, I applied on the spot, confident that this was the next step in my spiritual journey.

A few weeks later, an acceptance letter arrived. Despite my father's disapproval, I resigned from my job and packed my bags, fully committed to embracing all that God had in store for me.

NEW VISION

A year later, upon finishing school and returning home, I started to see my dad in a new light, viewing him through the eyes of the Father. It marked the beginning of our path toward healing and reconciliation. Our communication improved, even though we still occasionally had disagreements. Instead of taking offense, I responded from a higher perspective, which helped cultivate a greater understanding between us.

One day, I felt a prompting from the Holy Spirit to approach my dad and ask if I could sit on his lap, even though I was already an adult. In my heart, I sensed God was showing me that this symbolic act would be a catalyst for releasing the Father's love and bringing further healing to our relationship. Despite feeling uncomfortable, I moved forward with obedience. In that moment of vulnerability, God's presence met us, dissolving the barriers that had long stood between us.

This connection led to my dad supporting me in my ministry work. He even started attending the dream interpretation classes I taught at my church. Eagerly participating, he would sit in the front row, often being the first to offer answers to my questions.

The love of the Father not only fulfilled my deep emotional needs but also mended my relationship with my earthly father. Embracing His love allowed me to perceive my dad as a flawed human, much like myself, in need of love and acceptance. This shift from resentment to empathy led to more open and meaningful conversations between us. It also inspired me to share this love with others, reflecting God's love for all of us. That's the beauty of the Father's heart.

EMOTIONAL NEEDS OF THE HEART

The Bible refers to the heart almost a thousand times, which leads me to believe that the condition of our heart is critically important to God. Scripture explains that the heart is the part of us where our emotions dwell and plays a central role in motivating all our decisions. As Proverbs 4:23 (NAS) says, "Watch over your heart with all diligence, for from it flow the springs of life."

Our hearts thrive on three emotional needs: affection, affirmation, and attention, which are vital for nurturing a healthy sense of self and feeling loved. The deep-seated desire for unconditional love is intrinsic to our human nature. When we are truly seen, deeply valued, and genuinely appreciated, our hearts overflow with love, empowering us to fully embrace the joy of living.

This nurturing begins in the earliest stages of life, where parents are responsible for fulfilling their child's emotional needs, especially during the formative years. This foundation is critical for developing healthy relationships in adulthood. In particular, fathers play a vital role in shaping their children's identity and self-worth, making them feel safe and empowered for their mission in life.

The following examples illustrate how parents can fulfill these emotional needs:

- **Affection**—This need is met through physical gestures such as a warm embrace, a shoulder to lean on, a comforting touch, and verbal expressions, such as saying, "I love you" and "I miss you." By expressing care and devotion in these ways, parents effectively communicate affection for their children.

- **Affirmation**—This need is met by recognizing and praising a child's efforts, skills, talents, and giftings. Parents can nurture their child's future success by noticing and acknowledging their achievements. Offering affirming words such as "Great job" and "I am so proud of you!" can be very encouraging when they do something right.

- **Attention**—This need is met by being physically present, actively listening, engaging, and interacting. When a child asks their parents to watch them accomplish a new task, they seek their parent's time and attention. It's crucial for parents to intentionally spend time with their children and actively listen to them to show that they are valued and cared for.

If these emotional needs are not met, they may result in a feeling of deficiency or emptiness within the child, which demands attention. This void can persist into adulthood, potentially leading to the following conditions:

- **The Desperate Heart**—When a child does not receive the necessary attention and love from their parents, they may seek it in romantic relationships as they grow older. This quest for affection can lead to painful situations where individuals compromise their boundaries and self-respect, including engaging in sexual relationships, as they search for the love they missed from their parents.

- **The Codependent Heart**—Codependency often develops in those with unmet emotional needs during childhood. These individuals tend to become overly dependent on their relationships, sacrificing their own independence. They may tie their self-worth to their ability to meet the needs of others, neglecting their own desires and needs. This pattern can result in feelings of resentment and frustration, and in some cases, it can even contribute to the breakdown of marriages.

- **The Addicted Heart**—To fill the emotional void created by childhood neglect, some individuals turn to temporary pleasures such as food, shopping, sex, alcohol, or drugs. This behavior can lead to addiction as they seek relief from their unmet emotional needs through these substances or behaviors.

- **The Hopeless Heart**—A child who feels overlooked by their parents often struggles with loneliness and has difficulty forming meaningful friendships. This sense of emotional absence can potentially lead to conditions such as depression, anxiety, and fear. Individuals in this situation may internalize these feelings, blaming themselves for their emotional distress.

- **The Angry Heart**—Experiences of rejection, such as from parental divorce, favoritism, or scapegoating, can lead to long-lasting anger in individuals. This anger may manifest in self-destructive behaviors or harm toward others during adulthood to cope with the emotional pain of childhood neglect.

- **The Diseased Heart**—The persistent emotional stress resulting from unmet needs during childhood can increase the risk of physical health in adulthood. This stress can manifest as high blood pressure, ulcers, or other heart-related problems, highlighting the interconnectedness of emotional and physical well-being.

It's common for individuals to identify with one or more of these heart conditions, given that none of us had perfect parents or an ideal childhood. In reality, we all have hungry hearts, yet, as children of God, our emotional needs can be met by the love of our heavenly Father.

We can observe this truth beautifully demonstrated in Matthew 3:16-17 where even Jesus, who was perfect in every way, fulfilled His emotional needs by the Father during His baptism. First, the Father and the Holy Spirit were present at the event, giving Jesus their full attention.

Then the Father declared His love for Jesus by saying these words of affection, "This is My beloved Son," followed by these words of affirmation, "in whom I am well pleased." This event was a crucial turning point in Jesus' life and ministry, setting the course for His mission on earth.

THE SPIRIT OF ADOPTION

The parable of the Prodigal Son, found in Luke 15:11-32, vividly illustrates the Father's love in contrast to Jesus' baptism. Here, the focus shifts from a public mission declaration to a deeply personal story of a wayward son's acceptance by his father. The young man chooses to leave home against his father's guidance, demands his inheritance prematurely, and squanders it recklessly. Eventually, facing despair and poverty, he decides to return to his father, expecting to be treated as a servant.

The father not only accepts his son but does so with abundant love and joy, depicting our Heavenly Father's unconditional love and readiness to embrace us, regardless of our past mistakes or the condition of our hearts. Just as Jesus was affirmed and loved at His baptism, the Prodigal Son was welcomed back into the family, symbolizing the constant, renewing love of the Father available to all.

The young man's choices lead him to fear rejection and isolation, much like an orphan—devoid of family or belonging. Contrary to his expectations, his father warmly embraces him, signifying a profound shift from abandonment to welcome and restoration. This moment illustrates that his status as a son remains unchanged despite his past actions and detours.

This story parallels the biblical analogy of adoption in Romans 8:15 (NAS): "For you have not received a spirit of slavery leading to fear again, but you have received a spirit of adoption as sons *and daughters* by which we cry out, 'Abba! Father!'" This passage illuminates the intimate nature of our relationship with God, assuring us that we are not spiritual orphans. Instead, we are lovingly brought into God's family, embraced as His own children.

The spirit of adoption reshapes our perspective from viewing ourselves as lost or forsaken to realizing our precious position in God's heart. He is not distant but a caring Father who extends compassion and grace. Within this relationship, we discover our true identity and sense of belonging as cherished children of God, fully understood and profoundly loved.

Ephesians 1:5 (NAS) emphasizes that our adoption is not an afterthought, but a deliberate choice made by God: "He predestined us to adoption as sons *and daughters* through Jesus Christ to Himself, according to the good pleasure of His will." Through this adoption, we gain a new identity and inherit a promise of eternal belonging and love.

No matter your past experiences or the current state of your heart, you are always embraced by the nurturing love of our Heavenly Father. You are not left feeling like an orphan, abandoned, or overlooked. Whenever you call out to Him, saying "Abba! Father!" His immediate and unwavering unconditional love surrounds you. This love knows no bounds; it is wholehearted, ever-present, and overflowing with deep affection. It affirms your inherent potential and the unique purpose God has carefully designed for your life.

ACTIVATIONS

1. Reflect on your early years: Did you feel a lack of attention, affection, or affirmation? Can you identify with any of the "hungry heart" types that resonate with your past experiences?

2. What does "father" mean to you personally and spiritually? Take a moment today to immerse yourself in the Father's love. Acknowledge that you are His cherished child worthy of His love. Open your heart to receive and embrace His love.

CHAPTER 3

Discovering Your True Self

*"Define yourself radically as one beloved by God.
This is the true self. Every other identity is illusion."*
~Brennan Manning

FACING FEAR AND INSECURITY

While I was leading a women's ministry from my home, Melissa, a devoted member, approached me with a concern. She felt a strong calling to intercessory prayer, but the thought of speaking in front of others terrified her. Despite this, Melissa's desire to serve God and to make a meaningful impact in the lives of others was evident.

As Melissa shared her thoughts with me, I sensed that the root of her fear stemmed from childhood. After asking questions about her upbringing, Melissa opened up further about her past. She explained how her parents' tumultuous relationship led her to spend considerable time at her grandmother's house, a refuge where she felt loved, nurtured, and safe.

Tears welled up as Melissa recounted fond memories of her grandmother, who lovingly prepared her favorite meals, instilling a deep sense of comfort in food from an early age. This nurturing bond, however, led to a coping mechanism. Melissa eventually developed a habit of eating food whenever she felt stressed at home. Due to her weight, other family members often mocked her, causing her to feel rejected in her own home. This negative experience caused her to dislike her appearance so much that she usually avoided looking at herself in mirrors.

In recent years, Melissa's weight began to take a toll on her health, which forced her to change her lifestyle. With determination and hard work, she reached her goal weight and achieved a healthier appearance. Yet, despite her physical transformation, she continued to battle with insecurity and depression. It became evident to me that Melissa was still struggling with childhood rejection, and although she had lost the weight, she carried a spirit of heaviness.

SEEING THE TRUTH

Melissa believed in a distorted image of herself, but God wanted her to see the truth. She valued her time in prayer, explaining how she often received profound revelations about different people, nations, and world events, stirring her to intercede on their behalf. While Melissa was comfortable praying for individuals, privately or over the phone, she often hesitated to lead group prayers. Nevertheless, Melissa realized that it was time to move past her fears.

It became clear to me that this was a divine setup by God, as I had been asking Him to send intercessors to pray for the ministry's needs. The following week, Melissa found her opportunity to step into the role of a prayer leader. Her initial timidity transformed into growing confidence. As she voiced her heartfelt prayers, many were deeply touched and blessed by her powerful words. In answering her calling, Melissa brought her own prayers to life and became the answer to mine.

Melissa's transformation extended far beyond that prayer session. As her gift for intercession flourished, so did her confidence, impacting other areas of her life. She experienced a significant shift in perspective, and as a result, she began to see herself through God's eyes. This new outlook healed her strained family relationships and enhanced her capacity to love in ways she had never known. By accepting her true self, Melissa opened the door to a life filled with purpose and meaning.

A REFLECTION OF HIM

Melissa's story illustrates how a negative self-image can prevent us from realizing our full potential and sharing our talents with the world. While our individual experiences might vary, we all face challenges that can negatively impact how we see ourselves. Satan is no respecter of persons, and he will use any means to distort our self-perception. This relentless assault is driven by the enemy's hatred of seeing God's reflection in each of us.

The profound truth in Genesis 1:27 tells us that we are created in the image of God. This revelation affirms our worth and highlights the depths of His love for us. It invites us on a journey of self-discovery found in aligning with Jesus. As we center our thoughts and actions on Him, we gradually reflect His image more clearly.

A vital aspect of this journey is understanding our self-image, the mental picture we believe about our appearance, abilities, and personality. This image is primarily shaped by our personal experiences and the opinions of others that we've internalized. However, our perception may not necessarily reflect our true identity accurately; often, there's a disconnect between how we see ourselves and who we are in the eyes of God. To bridge this gap, we must recognize these discrepancies and actively seek to align our perception with God's view of us.

During my mentoring sessions, I sometimes guide individuals through exercises that examine their self-perception. An effective method involves having them look into a mirror while asking themselves questions like, "How do I see myself?" and "Who am I?" This practice often reveals layers of personal thoughts and beliefs that shape their identity.

It's important to understand that our self-image is not static; it can change over time due to our experiences and interactions with others. The accuracy of this image depends on the "mirror" we choose to look into. Mirrors tainted by negative experiences can lead to an unhealthy self-image, whereas a mirror reflecting God's truth provides a more accurate and affirming view.

For this reason, regular evaluation of our self-image is essential for spiritual growth. Imagine using a scale from one to ten, where one represents a highly distorted self-perception and ten reflects alignment with God's perspective. This introspective approach helps ensure that our self-image aligns with our true self, leading us to reflect the characteristics of Jesus in our daily lives.

Factors that can influence our self-image include:

- **Relationships**—Our interactions, particularly with family members and influential figures, profoundly shape our self-perception. Parents, for example, play a pivotal role from birth, with their words and actions serving as the primary mirror. As we grow and develop, this circle expands to include teachers, relatives, and friends, each playing a part in our evolving self-perception.

- **Judgments and Expectations**—Growing up in environments filled with criticism and unrealistic expectations can lead to internalizing negative labels, resulting in an unhealthy self-image. During childhood, we are especially susceptible to such judgments from authority figures, often leading to a focus on our weaknesses and imperfections.

- **Emotional and Physical Harm**—Traumatic experiences of abuse, neglect, or manipulation can severely damage our self-image, trapping us in feelings of guilt, shame, and self-blame, which can lead to depression, hopelessness, and despair. Overcoming these situations requires seeking healing and counseling to embrace a healthier self-image.

- **Culture**— The beliefs and values we are exposed to during our upbringing significantly influence our self-perception. The portrayal of unrealistic standards for beauty and success in the media often leads to unfavorable comparisons and dissatisfaction. We must recognize that these cultural norms often do not align with deeper spiritual truths about our identity and who God says we are.

While external validation can contribute to a positive self-image, it is not sufficient in itself. Relying solely on the support of parents and role models can confine us to their expectations and opinions. A thorough and lasting sense of self is established by looking beyond human validation and actively seeking God's perspective. This pursuit leads us to discover the unique individuals He designed us to be.

NEW CREATIONS IN CHRIST

As followers of Christ, we find our true identity by looking to Jesus as our mirror. He not only reveals our purpose but also the distinct qualities that define us. 2 Corinthians 3:18 (NAS) beautifully illustrates this process, "But we all, with unveiled face, looking as in a mirror at the glory of the Lord, are being transformed into the same image from glory to glory, just as from the Lord, the Spirit." This verse emphasizes that the more we focus on Jesus, the more we are shaped into His image by the Holy Spirit.

The transformation we experience in Christ is captured by the Greek word *metamorphoo*, which means "metamorphosis," the term used to illustrate the remarkable process of caterpillars becoming butterflies.[ii] While religion can sometimes lead us to believe that we are bound to our old, flawed selves, the message of Jesus' sacrifice on the cross tells us otherwise. We are completely renewed through Christ, no longer bound by our past imperfections.

Like a butterfly emerging from a cocoon, we gradually shed the characteristics of our old nature and emerge as a new creation, reflecting the beauty and freedom of God's glory. 2 Corinthians 5:17 (NKJV) states, "Therefore, if anyone is in Christ, he is a new creation; old things have passed away; behold, all things have become new."

This transformation is comprehensive, affecting every aspect of life. Embracing a new identity in Christ doesn't mean losing our uniqueness or individuality. Instead, we shed what distances us from God, adopting a life that is impactful and exemplifies the character and love of Jesus.

This new identity transcends our past experiences and cultural backgrounds. As we align with Jesus and His righteousness, Colossians 3:3 states that we are "hidden" in Christ, meaning when God looks at us, He no longer sees our old sinful self. Instead, He sees us as perfect in Jesus. However, embracing this truth can be challenging.

When we look in the mirror, the enemy often tries to draw our attention to our failures and flaws, leading us to self-doubt. He knows that if we don't like what we see, it will become more and more challenging to see ourselves as God does. This focus can lead us to question, "Am I good enough? Do I have what it takes? Am I truly worthy?"

In moments of doubt, the Word of God provides the answers we need. As John 1:1-3 reveals, Jesus is the Word made flesh. He affirms our identity by declaring that we are masterpieces (Ephesians 2:10), fearfully and wonderfully made (Psalm 139:14), and highly valued (1 John 3:21). Our past, pain, and cultural background do not define us; it is God's Word that does.

To help you deepen your understanding and acceptance of your true self, consider these practical steps:

- **Visualize Jesus**—Imagine Jesus smiling at you and saying, "I love you." Reflect on the emotions this visualization brings.

- **Dialog with Jesus**—In prayer, ask Jesus to reveal how He sees you. Afterward, journal your thoughts, feelings, or any impressions you believe are from God.

- **Mirror Exercise with Scriptures**—Select Bible verses that resonate with your true identity and post them on your mirror. Recite these verses, personalizing them as affirmations about yourself.

- **Self-Affirmation and Acceptance**—Conclude your practice by looking at yourself in the mirror and affirming yourself with the words, "I love you." Embrace this moment of self-acceptance and recognition of your true self.

By incorporating these exercises into your daily routine, you will begin to recognize your true self as God sees you. These methods are practical and have been effective for many people, including individuals like Melissa, who have overcome struggles with their self-image.

JACOB'S TRANSFORMATION

Jacob's life, as depicted in the Bible, serves as a compelling illustration of personal transformation. As the younger twin in his family, he often sought approval, particularly from his mother, Rebekah. Under her influence, Jacob frequently resorted to deception to achieve his desires.

A critical turning point occurs in Genesis 27 when Jacob, disguised as his brother, Esau, deceives his father, Isaac, into giving him the blessing intended for his elder sibling. This act of deceit forces Jacob to flee his home, marking the beginning of a profound journey of self-discovery and transformation.

While away from home, Jacob's interactions with his cunning father-in-law, Laban, led him to ponder his own behavior. This self-reflection prompted Jacob to reconsider the person he wanted to be and rethink his identity.

A wrestling match with God marks the pivotal moment in Jacob's journey. This intense struggle was more than a physical confrontation; it symbolized Jacob's internal battle with his past decisions and identity. Emerging from this encounter, Jacob is transformed both physically and spiritually. He receives a new name, Israel, indicating a significant shift in his identity. This change of name symbolized a transition from a life characterized by manipulation (Jacob) to one marked by empowerment and alignment with God's kingdom purpose (Israel).

Jacob's story is a timeless message that speaks to each of us today. Much like Jacob, we all carry the potential for transformation and growth. Take a moment to reflect on your own life. Are you living in the fullness of your authentic self, enjoying God's blessings and freedom, or do you feel restricted by the expectations and roles imposed on you by others?

Discovering your true self involves letting go of past mistakes and misunderstandings that may have hindered you and accepting your new identity with unwavering faith. Through this process, you will rise with purpose and confidence, becoming a beacon of God's love and grace in a world that desperately needs it.

ACTIVATIONS

1. Look into the mirror and write down what you see. Be honest, and include any thoughts, feelings, and reflections on how you see yourself and who you believe you truly are. Practice the steps outlined in this chapter daily until you recognize your true self in the mirror.

2. Do you have any areas in your life where you are seeking transformation or change? How can "wrestling with God" and facing your challenges head-on help you embrace your true identity and purpose?

Finding Confidence by Knowing Your Worth

"We don't need self-confidence,
we need God-confidence."
Joyce Meyer

OUT OF THE SHADOWS

Cathleen, a student in one of my online courses, contacted me for a one-on-one coaching session. During our conversation, she expressed her deep-seated fear of sharing her talents with the world, a feeling that resonated with my own experiences, having faced similar challenges myself. Cathleen had a unique gift for songwriting, yet she was grappling with anxiety and uncertainty about releasing her songs to a broader audience.

Cathleen's life took an extraordinary turn during her teenage years as she found herself under the wing of her uncle, an internationally famous musician known to many. Working as his assistant, a job she cherished, she traveled the world on tours, absorbing the exciting variety of cultures and the lively world of music. However, as she matured, Cathleen began to feel the urge to step out from under her uncle's shadow and carve her own path in life.

Eventually, Cathleen transitioned to an office job, seeking the stability and income it promised. Yet, this new chapter came with its own set of challenges. The long work hours and constant stress began to take a toll on her health, resulting in high blood pressure and a growing disconnection from her true passion for music and songwriting. Additionally, the looming shadow of her uncle's fame made her hesitant to share her talents and pursue opportunities due to the fear of comparison.

As her coach, I had the privilege of helping Cathleen rebuild her confidence. We developed a clear, actionable plan tailored to help her realize her dreams. Cathleen focused on taking small, intentional steps each day to confront her insecurities. She began to acknowledge her worth and put her faith in God, trusting in His guidance to realize her dreams.

This gradual process led to a remarkable transformation in Cathleen. She took charge of her health, refusing to wait for the "perfect" moment to act. With steady determination, Cathleen found her distinctive voice and gained the courage to pursue singing and speaking opportunities. Moreover, Cathleen began documenting her life's journey in a book, becoming an inspiration for others. Today, Cathleen lives a happier, healthier life, actively pursuing her dreams with a clear sense of purpose.

TO TRUST

Confidence profoundly influences our relationships, work, and ability to trust in ourselves and others. Despite its crucial role in our lives, many find this quality challenging to attain. Interestingly, the word confidence comes from the Latin term *fidere*, meaning "to trust."[iii]

The world often encourages us to place our trust in personal resources, abilities, and strengths to build confidence. For instance, many individuals may find confidence in their wealth, while others may rely on their professional status, and some may find it in their physical appearance. However, these sources are temporary and can fluctuate or diminish, which can lead to wavering or lost confidence.

In contrast, placing our trust in God, who is eternal, provides a steadfast source of confidence. This doesn't mean that God opposes us having wealth or success. Rather, it's about prioritizing our confidence in Him above all else. As Jeremiah 17:7 (GW) states, "Blessed is the person who trusts the Lord. The Lord will be his confidence."

Our level of confidence is directly tied to our self-esteem, shaping how we perceive ourselves. The term esteem comes from the Latin word *aestimare*, which means "to assess or value."[iv] When we struggle with low confidence, it often signifies deeper issues with our self-esteem, which arise from our failure to appreciate our inherent value and worth. In such situations, we tend to be overly critical, fixating on perceived flaws rather than acknowledging our strengths and untapped potential.

We can avoid much pain and suffering by changing where we seek validation. Instead of relying on external sources, we should find assurance in the profound worth and value that only God can provide. This shift in perspective allows us to be grounded, with a stable and unwavering self-esteem and confidence.

M.V.P.

Throughout Scripture, God repeatedly affirms our worth. We find declarations like being described as a crown of glory and a royal diadem in His hand in Isaiah 62:3, reminders in Psalm 139:16 of how all our days are preordained and noted by God before they even begin, and assurances in Ephesians 1:11 about our inheritance in heaven as His children. These affirmations highlight that we are considered His most valuable possessions, a status granted by the price Jesus paid to make us worthy.

John 3:16 (ESV) reinforces this truth: "For God so loved the world, that he gave his only Son, that whoever believes in him should not perish but have eternal life." This profound expression of love helps us grasp our true worth in Him, leading to a deep trust in God and, consequently, in ourselves. Sustained by the Holy Spirit within, this trust guides us confidently toward our predetermined destinies, filled with abundant life.

As our confidence grows, it's not uncommon to still face insecurity and self-esteem challenges. Yet, we can take comfort in the understanding that perfection isn't required. Our weaknesses should lead us to greater dependence upon God.

On such occasions, we can turn to 2 Corinthians 12:9 for reassurance where Paul recounts God's words to him: "My grace is sufficient for you, for my power is made perfect in weakness." These times of vulnerability present valuable opportunities to nurture our trust in God, allowing His power to be revealed in and through us.

BUILDING SELF-ESTEEM

Self-esteem plays a significant role in shaping our thoughts, actions, and emotions. When our esteem is firmly rooted in God, it not only empowers us with the strength and flexibility needed to take charge of our lives but also allows us to learn and grow from our mistakes without fearing rejection. This awareness encourages us to step out of our comfort zone, pursue new opportunities, and establish meaningful connections.

Building and maintaining self-esteem is an ongoing process. It involves constant reminders that our value stems from being children of God. Without finding our worth in Him, we risk developing personality types characterized by low self-esteem, such as:

- **The Perfectionist, High Achiever, Competitive, or "Type A" Personality**—People in this category often find their worth in achievements. Setting excessively high standards for success, they frequently encounter disappointment and a sense of failure; this leads to a fear of not meeting expectations, resulting in procrastination and a vicious cycle that further diminishes their self-esteem.

- **The Fearful (Frozen) Personality**—These individuals avoid risks and prefer playing it safe, much like the man in the parable of the talents (Matthew 25:14-30), who buried his talent due to feelings of inadequacy and fear. Suffering from "analysis paralysis," they become trapped in overthinking and hesitancy, preventing them from taking action and stepping out in faith. Their talents and potential become frozen assets, leading to a life of stagnation.

- **The Mistrusting Personality**—People in this group are often skeptical about being loved. They respond to low self-esteem by withdrawing from relationships, allowing their misperception of themselves to taint their view of others. This mistrust results in building walls to avoid getting hurt. They end up exactly where Satan wants them, isolated from God and others.

- **The Indecisive Personality**—A person in this category has difficulty making decisions and often prefers others due to a lack of trust in making the right choices. As described in James 1:8, this leads to a "double-minded" state, causing instability and a lack of clear direction in life.

- **The Defensive Personality**—These individuals react aggressively to perceived criticism, often resorting to excuses or blaming others. Their responses vary from irritation to contentious, reflecting a lack of confidence and avoidance of personal accountability. They often see themselves as victims rather than victors in challenging situations.

A lack of self-esteem can also lead to problems such as insecurity, jealousy, anger, selfishness, guilt, pride, and feelings of inferiority. Ultimately, these issues lead to a purposeless life, wasted gifts, and unfulfilled dreams. They are also significant contributors to depression.

Pause and consider if any of these personality types resonate with you. It's quite normal to struggle with one or more of these characteristics occasionally. Remember, the key is to concentrate on your continuous growth, as transformation is a journey—not a one-time event.

To help build your self-esteem and trust in God, here are some practical solutions:

- **Aim for excellence, not perfection**—Focus on doing your best, recognizing that improvement comes with practice. When the goal is perfection, tasks often remain unfinished. Remember, your ultimate goal is to please God through your endeavors, as stated in Colossians 3:23 (ESV): "Whatever you do, work heartily, as for the Lord and not for men," reminding us that it's your sincere dedication, not flawlessness, that truly counts.

- **Take a risk**—God often leads us out of our comfort zone, as illustrated in Matthew 14:29 (GW), "Jesus said 'Come!' So Peter got out of the boat and walked on the water toward Jesus." Give yourself permission to stumble and fall along the way, knowing that everyone makes mistakes. The important thing is to get back up and try again.

- **Be yourself**—Embrace your true self, and don't allow external factors to dictate your identity. Your worth comes from within and should not rely on outside approval. God created you uniquely to give and receive love. If someone rejects you, it doesn't diminish your worth. Instead, surround yourself with people who appreciate and support the real you. Find encouragement in Hebrews 13:6 (NLT), which reads: "So we can say with confidence, 'The LORD is my helper, so I will have no fear. What can mere people do to me?'"

- **Commit to your goals**—Seek wisdom and direction from God as you set your objectives. Follow peace in your decisions, make firm choices, and stick to them. Trust that God is guiding you to manage situations and tasks effectively. Proverbs 16:3 (ESV) reinforces this approach: "Commit your work to the LORD, and your plans will be established."

- **Take responsibility for your actions and behavior**—Ask God for insight into what you can learn in every situation. This approach to accountability fosters wisdom and growth. Proverbs 4:11 (NIV) supports this, saying, "I instruct you in the way of wisdom and lead you along straight paths."

LESSONS FROM GIDEON

The Bible story of Gideon illustrates his ongoing struggle with confidence and self-esteem. It starts in Judges 6 with God calling Gideon to free Israel from the Midianites, addressing him as a "mighty warrior." Gideon doubted his capabilities by questioning, "How can I save Israel? My clan is the weakest in Manasseh, and I am the youngest in my family." This response highlights a common human tendency to focus on our perceived weaknesses rather than trusting in God's strength.

Plagued with self-doubt, Gideon asked God for a sign to confirm His calling—not once, not twice, but three times. Even after God provided miraculous signs, Gideon obeyed God's command to tear down his father's altar of Baal, but he did so cautiously, fearing the opinions of others. Later, God demonstrated His might again by granting Gideon and his mere three hundred men victory over 135,000 Midianites.

Instead of honoring God, Gideon's actions shifted toward arrogance. He created a golden ephod from their collected spoils, leading Israel to sin by idol worship. Gideon's journey from low self-esteem to the other extreme of pride highlights the danger of not finding our worth in God. Despite his victory, Gideon grappled with placing his trust in God, leading him to claim for himself the glory that rightfully belonged to God.

Gideon's story serves as an important reminder: self-esteem and confidence should stem from an internal relationship with God, not from outward successes. Failing to recognize this can lead to the same prideful downfall Gideon experienced.

Take a moment to reflect on your motivations for success. It's common for confidence derived from worldly achievements to be driven by selfish ambition. In contrast, confidence built through faith in God cultivates a right relationship with Him and is essential for unlocking the extraordinary plan He has for your life.

Therefore, when God calls you to a task that seems larger than life, rest assured that He has a purpose and equips you with the power to fulfill it. Despite any feelings of inadequacy, God doesn't require you to rely on your strength. Instead, He desires your wholehearted trust in Him without a backup plan.

This aligns with Proverbs 3:5-6 (NAS), which advises, "Trust in the LORD with all your heart and do not lean on your own understanding. In all your ways acknowledge Him, and He will make your paths straight." This scripture reinforces your identity as a cherished child of the Father, deserving of His love and an exceptional calling. Trusting in God involves embracing the unknown with faith. By placing your confidence in Him, you open the way for His guidance to lead you to a life of abundance and purpose.

ACTIVATIONS

1. Can you relate to any of the low self-esteem person-
    alities listed? Which ones and why?

2. Pick a God solution that you can apply to a current
    situation that you are facing to help build your confi-
    dence and worth. Journal the steps you take and the
    results you see.

3. Have you ever faced a situation in your life where you felt inadequate, like Gideon? If so, how did you respond, and what lessons can you draw from Gideon's journey about trusting in God and finding confidence in Him, even when facing self-doubt?

CHAPTER 5

Renewing Your Mind

*"God designed humans to observe our own thoughts,
catch those that are bad, and get rid of them."*
~Carolyn Leaf

THE MIRACLE PUPPY

After months of searching for the perfect addition to our family, I stumbled upon the puppy we'd been looking for. Everything aligned perfectly, or so it appeared. Months earlier, my husband, Gus, and I had already planned a trip to Los Angeles, and to our surprise, this was precisely where we found the puppy.

Upon contacting the seller, we were happy to learn that the puppy would be available for pick-up the same weekend we'd be there. It felt like a true blessing; things fell into place seamlessly, as if orchestrated by God.

This puppy happened to be a rare "designer" breed, and it came with a price tag to match. Initially, I hesitated, never having spent so much on a pet. Yet, the breed's uniqueness and stunning color ultimately persuaded me. To make it an extra special surprise, we decided to wait until we returned home to reveal our new family member to the children.

While in Los Angeles, we took care of all the required payments and paperwork to bring our new furry addition home. However, we had to wait until his scheduled vaccination, which was on the last day of our trip. With limited time that day and a flight to catch, we hurried to meet the seller. Yet, to my shock and astonishment, the puppy she handed me was not the same one I had seen in the pictures! I was in utter disbelief—I had fallen victim to a scam!

There was no time to argue; we could not risk being late for our flight. A deep sense of disappointment overwhelmed me. What was meant to be an exciting moment swiftly turned into frustration, triggering feelings of resentment toward the seller, myself, and even the poor dog.

While on our return flight, I was scrolling through the photos Gus had taken during our trip when a particular image caught my eye. It was a picture of me holding the puppy, with a rainbow on his face! I had never seen anything like it and couldn't help but think it was a sign of hope from God.

Before drifting off to sleep that night, I couldn't help but reflect on how the dog incident was just another setback in the relentless series of challenges I had faced over the past few years. Negative thoughts flooded my mind, and I realized I needed to take control over them before they consumed me. At that moment, I chose to surrender the situation to God.

As the first light of dawn appeared, I sensed the Holy Spirit's gentle nudge, encouraging me to rise and pray. He directed me to the story of Job, igniting my faith and instilling in me the belief that just as Job was restored double, God would do the same for me.

NEW BEGINNING

Later that day, Gus shared an unusual discovery with me: a two-dollar bill in our front yard—a notable find due to its rarity. Instantly, the story of Job, which I had read earlier that morning, came to mind. I frequently receive confirmations of God's messages to me through signs, which became even more evident when this strange event repeated itself for the next three days. Remarkably, my husband found a two-dollar bill in our front yard for four consecutive days.

As he handed me the bills, totaling eight dollars—a number symbolizing "new beginnings"—I couldn't ignore the clear message from God. This sign confirmed over and over what I had been sensing: I was entering a new season filled with renewal and hope.

I decided to completely trust in God's Word, no longer allowing the negative thoughts to discourage me. Holding onto His promise of restoration, I witnessed numerous blessings returning to my life. The puppy brought immense joy to my family, and through the disappointments, I've learned that God is faithful and continually works things out for the better.

EVALUATING YOUR SELF-TALK

Our thoughts are powerful, capable of either propelling us toward success or dragging us into despair. When rooted in truth, they guide us on the right path. However, without this foundation, there's a risk of being led astray into deception. To address this, we must regularly evaluate our self-talk—the continuous stream of unspoken thoughts that flow through our minds.

What we think and say to ourselves significantly influences our outlook. Focusing on the negative often leads us to perceive the glass as half empty, whereas a naturally optimistic view sees it as half full. However, even a positive mindset can waver in challenging times. That's why it's essential to seek God's perspective, which is filled with hope and goodness.

We should believe that every good aspect of our lives originates from God, as affirmed in James 1:17. This verse reminds us of our unchanging heavenly Father, whose goodness persists even through our trials. The gospel message powerfully illustrates this goodness, primarily through God sending His only Son, Jesus, to make the ultimate sacrifice on the cross. This sacrificial love stands as a testament to our ability to trust in God, regardless of our circumstances, knowing that He consistently acts for our ultimate benefit.

Romans 8:28 offers further assurance that God can bring good out of any situation, no matter how awful it may seem. His ways are beyond our own, requiring us to seek understanding through His Word.

The Bible contains numerous verses about the mind and our thought processes. Proverbs 4:23, for instance, urges us to guard our thoughts as they shape our lives. In other words, whatever we focus on influences our actions and, ultimately, determines our destiny.

Negative self-talk can be particularly damaging, gradually leading us down an unwanted path. In such situations, we should pause and remember that the Holy Spirit dwells within us, giving us the strength to conquer these harmful thought patterns. Without Him, we are left defenseless.

BE LED BY THE SPIRIT

Many of us let our emotions govern our thoughts, yet it's important to recognize that emotions are part of our physical nature and can sometimes lead us astray. Romans 8:6 (NAS) captures this concept well: "For the mind set on the flesh is death, but the mind set on the Spirit is life and peace." God intends emotions to serve as indicators, providing information rather than direction. As Jeremiah 17:9 cautions, our hearts are inherently deceitful, implying that our feelings are not always trustworthy. However, under the guidance of the Holy Spirit, our emotions can become valuable tools for our spiritual growth.

Satan is aware of our weaknesses and often exploits our emotions to tempt us. Since our feelings are susceptible to various external influences, like too much caffeine or not enough sleep, we cannot rely on them as a source for decision-making. Instead, seeking the Holy Spirit, who consistently leads us toward the truth, is a much wiser approach.

Aligning our daily decisions with God's will empowers us to walk in His strength and victory. By yielding to the Holy Spirit's promptings, teachings, and guidance, we become equipped to resist worldly temptations. The Apostle Paul reinforces this in Galatians 5:16, urging believers to "walk by the Spirit" to overcome the desire of the flesh, therefore shaping a life that reflects God's glory and truth.

KNOWING GOD'S THOUGHTS

The mind is where our emotions, thoughts, and decisions converge, defining our inner world. It's also the battlefield where truth and lies continually clash. In this ongoing spiritual battle, Satan actively seeks to gain ground by sowing thoughts that contradict the truth, hindering us from experiencing God's promises. It's important to remember that we're not alone in this struggle—everyone faces it. To prevail, we must be vigilant and discerning about the thoughts we allow to take root in our minds.

The thoughts we internalize become our truth and influence our decisions. Paul tells us in 1 Corinthians 2:16 that we have been given the mind of Christ through salvation. The Holy Spirit within us illuminates Scripture and gives us access to the wisdom and insight of Christ. To fully embrace this mindset, effort on our part is required.

Romans 12:2 further reinforces this idea, emphasizing the need for a transformation that begins in the mind. This transformation is achieved through the renewal of our thoughts—a process that involves changing our thinking patterns to reflect spiritual truths. Engaging in the discipline of renewal is essential for discerning God's will and living a purposeful, fulfilling life that honors Him.

The key to knowing what God is thinking and saying lies in His Word. That's why we should cultivate a daily habit of reading our Bibles. This practice is vital for aligning our thoughts with those of God. As Ephesians 5:26 illustrates, Christ purifies us into His image through the cleansing power of His Word.

Engaging in this renewal process leads to swift, positive life changes. It can free us from the enemy's grip, allowing us to view life from a higher perspective through the lens of God. To participate in this transformative journey, we must be intentional. The enemy won't easily give up ground, and he constantly bombards our minds with lies that oppose God's thoughts.

We are instructed by Paul in 2 Corinthians 10:5 (ESV) to "destroy arguments and every lofty opinion raised against the knowledge of God, and take every thought captive to obey Christ." This proactive approach involves confronting and challenging every thought that opposes the truth. We triumph in this battle by mastering our thoughts, ensuring they adhere to God's Word. However, failure to actively manage our thoughts can allow them to grow unchecked, potentially developing into ungodly beliefs and strongholds (which we will discuss in the next chapter).

BREAKING NEGATIVE MINDSETS AND THOUGHT PATTERNS

It's surprising to see how many people attend church regularly yet still have negative mindsets, living in a state of stress and worry. As believers, we have the Holy Spirit, who helps us align our thoughts with God, thereby positioning us to experience all the blessings He has prepared for us, regardless of any negative thought patterns we may have learned in the past.

Ephesians 4:22-24 (ESV) instructs us to "put off your old self, which belongs to your former manner of life and is corrupt through deceitful desires, and to be renewed in the spirit of your minds, and to put on the new self, created after the likeness of God in true righteousness and holiness."

As we work to bring our thoughts into obedience, we will encounter resistance from our "old self." The struggle is relentless, demanding our steadfast commitment, as the enemy is persistent. Failing to engage in this spiritual battle or surrendering to it allows our sinful nature to assume control over our thought life.

God desires us to lead a life abundant in hope and joy, even when facing difficult circumstances. In times of adversity, it's essential to shield our minds from the negative thoughts sown by Satan, as they can disrupt our inner peace. Instead, focus on God's thoughts, which lead to a wholesome life. With the mind of Christ, we can navigate life's trials with grace and strength.

The following steps offer simple yet powerful solutions to help you break free from negative thought patterns and cultivate the mind of Christ:

- **Reflect Instead of React**—In challenging moments, choose reflection over despair. Learn from your experiences and seek God's insight into negative reactions to avoid spiraling into destructive thoughts.

- **Take Responsibility for Your Life**—Conquer hindrances like blame and self-pity. Regardless of past events, you can overcome with God's assistance. By accepting responsibility and following God's guidance, you will see the changes you desire. Remember, you are not a victim.

- **Examine Your Soul**—Seek the Holy Spirit's guidance in uncovering any negative emotions within you, such as fear, pride, envy, anger, or selfishness, as they can influence your thoughts and perspectives. Confess and turn away from them, inviting God's transformative power to bring about change within you.

- **Recognize and Reframe Negative Thoughts**—Whenever negative emotions arise, pause to identify and counter the underlying thought with God's truth. Actively engage in aligning your thoughts with the Word of God.

God's incredible promises await you, but you must fight to claim them in your mind. Attaining a "new self" demands consistent, deliberate action. By diligently immersing yourself in God's Word day by day, you will gradually begin to see the world through His perspective.

Even when life brings unexpected disappointments, hold onto the assurance of God's unwavering faithfulness. He continuously works for your good. With the mind of Christ, you'll make decisions rooted in wisdom and discernment, paving the way to the abundant life He lovingly intends for you—one overflowing with His grace, purpose, and everlasting joy.

ACTIVATIONS

1. Consider a negative emotion you often feel, such as anger, sadness, fear, jealousy, or any other. Identify any thoughts connected to that emotion, and then search for a relevant Bible verse that counters those thoughts. Use it as your go-to response whenever you encounter that particular emotion.

2. Reflect on a recent disappointment you experienced. What was your initial reaction? What did you learn from it? Seek God's perspective and journal your reflections.

CHAPTER 6

Breaking Free from Ungodly Beliefs

*"Whether you think you can,
or think you can't, you're right."*
~Henry Ford

FINDING THE ROOT

I received a distressing call from Natalie, one of my coaching clients, who urgently requested prayer regarding her job. She explained that her manager had issued a verbal warning about her work performance. Although she was given an opportunity to improve, Natalie felt undervalued and contemplated looking for a job where she could feel more appreciated.

Natalie had encountered these feelings in previous positions. Upon further exploration, she shared an incident from early in her career when her boss unjustly terminated her. Nevertheless, I sensed that the underlying issue ran deeper than that.

With the intention of getting to the root of the issue, we prayed and sought the Holy Spirit's guidance to help uncover a memory that first triggered these feelings in Natalie. She immediately recalled an incident from her childhood where her dad harshly disciplined her for not making good grades on her report card. She explained how her father often unfavorably compared her to her older sister, who was an honor roll student. This memory revealed a recurring pattern: Natalie associated meeting expectations with love and acceptance while falling short was linked to feelings of failure and disappointment.

Natalie's "black-and-white" thinking, which involves seeing things in extremes, was evident in how she handled criticism at work. Instead of viewing her manager's feedback as constructive, she saw it as confirmation of being inadequate. It led her to equate meeting expectations with being "good" and any shortfall with being "bad," with no room for improvement. This type of thinking is a common defense mechanism used by people who have experienced trauma, especially during their childhood.

As a result, Natalie internalized her manager's feedback, leading her to perceive herself as a poor employee. Instead of using the opportunity to enhance her performance, Natalie began searching for another job, fearing termination. This thought pattern, deeply rooted in her past, profoundly impacted her emotional well-being and hindered her success in her current role.

BREAKING THE CYCLE

Throughout our sessions, we tackled the mindset pattern that had been affecting Natalie's career and personal life. We focused on addressing the childhood trauma and challenging the false beliefs, systematically dismantling the strongholds they had formed. Consequently, Natalie achieved the breakthrough she needed to align herself with God's plan for her life.

Natalie's breakthrough helped her stay committed to her job, which paved the way to significant professional and personal development. She was able to welcome feedback as an avenue for growth, which eventually earned her recognition and also led to her promotion as a consultant. This role opened doors to specialized training and certification.

The success she found in her current job has given her the courage to start a side business as a leadership and life coach. This endeavor has brought her much joy and fulfillment as she is helping others grow personally and in their businesses.

CONFRONTING THE LIE AND THE LIAR

It's natural to feel upset and defensive when we discover someone is spreading false information about us. However, the situation becomes more complex when we realize the source of these lies is our thoughts, taking the form of ungodly beliefs. These self-deceptive thoughts often remain hidden and unnoticed, silently influencing our self-perception.

Ungodly beliefs are the lies we tell ourselves that contradict the truth found in the Word of God. Such beliefs originate from the fall of mankind in the Garden of Eden, as depicted in Genesis 3:1-7. In this story, Satan tempts Eve by distorting God's words, planting seeds of doubt in her mind about God's love and truth for her. At this moment, she faced a choice between believing Satan, the father of lies, or God, the One who is Truth.

Today, Satan continues to use the same tactics by planting lies to deceive people. The enemy often launches these assaults during our formative years when we are most vulnerable and impressionable. Childhood traumas and negative experiences can leave a lasting impact, leading to the adoption of ungodly beliefs that can affect our entire lives and ultimately shape our identity.

These ungodly beliefs, also referred to as limiting beliefs, have the power to delay our personal growth, preventing us from becoming who we are meant to be. Think of them as a stretched rubber band, taking us only so far, then swiftly retracting us back to our starting point, thereby limiting our actions and hindering us from reaching our full potential.

Within these beliefs, we often find inner vows—self-imposed promises that emerge in response to painful experiences, usually containing the words "never" or "always." For example, if we believe the lie, "I am not good enough," we might make inner vows such as, "I will always work harder to prove my worth," or "I will never take risks to avoid failure."

The first step toward breaking free from the grip of these limiting beliefs is to acknowledge and confront them. If left unchallenged, they gradually embed themselves in our minds, forming a stronghold that influences our actions.

STRONGHOLDS

Our thoughts play a powerful role in shaping our identity, as Proverbs 23:7 (NKJV) highlights: "For as he thinks in his heart, so is he." Essentially, we become what we consistently focus on. Therefore, when we believe what God says about us, it becomes evident in our lives. Conversely, if we continually dwell on lies about ourselves, we may find ourselves trapped in a recurring pattern of pain or sin, making it seemingly impossible to break free—a potential sign of a mental stronghold.

These strongholds dictate our actions by creating a belief-expectation-behavior-experience cycle. They compel us to act on expectations rooted in distorted perceptions and feelings, further reinforcing these beliefs through our experiences. Until we face the lie underlying these strongholds, we will continue to experience circumstances that seem to confirm it, and every time, we will believe the lie to be true, perpetuating the cycle.

Strongholds may form due to negative or traumatic experiences dating back as far as our time in our mother's womb. They can be passed down through generations, learned from our surroundings, or rooted in personal experiences. Ultimately, strongholds will draw us to the same or similar situations repeatedly, causing us more grief and pain.

Resistant to change, a stronghold is a stubborn mindset that can be challenging to break free from. However, after being trapped in these cycles of pain and suffering for an extended period, we may reach a point where we become aware of the harm we are causing ourselves and finally decide to make a change.

In military terms, a stronghold is a fortified or hiding place.[v] Imagine that each time we believe a lie, it's as if we're laying down a brick, eventually building a wall within our minds. Behind this wall, the enemy gains territory, staying hidden. As discussed in the previous chapter, a fierce battle persists in our minds between the kingdom of God and the kingdom of Satan. The enemy's ultimate goal is to have complete dominion over our souls, gaining control over our thoughts, willpower, and emotions.

2 Corinthians 10:4 (ESV) states, "For the weapons of our warfare are not of the flesh but have divine power to destroy strongholds," meaning we cannot rely on our strength to tear down these demonic strongholds but on the power of God's Word.

Strongholds must be dismantled brick by brick. Every time we confront a lie with the truth of God's Word, we remove a brick, and as we continue to do so, the enemy is left with nowhere to hide. He eventually loses ground in our minds and can no longer control our thoughts.

However, it is not enough to simply eliminate ungodly beliefs. We must also establish new, godly beliefs rooted in truth to both guard against the enemy and to open ourselves to the blessings and opportunities God has for us. Adopting these new beliefs, which align with our true identity, requires unwavering commitment and dedication.

EMBRACING GODLY BELIEFS

When we have spent a lifetime believing lies, we must give ourselves grace and time to change. In 1960, psychologist Maxwell Maltz, author of "Psycho-Cybernetics," conducted a study. [vi] He found that forming a new habit took a minimum of twenty-one days. This insight should remind us to be patient with ourselves as we work through this process, with repetition and consistency being essential elements.

Confronting ungodly beliefs is often an ongoing process, as new challenges tend to emerge. From my personal experience and in mentoring others, it's evident that these struggles are common to us all. Satan's deceptions can lead us to believe his lies, making us feel as though we are the only ones wrestling with these thoughts. But I want to assure you that you are not alone.

The following is a list of common ungodly beliefs, along with examples of godly beliefs to help you counter the lies with God's truth:

I can't be my real self, or I'll be judged.

There will always be people in your life who will judge you. Everyone has the right to their own opinions, and it's impossible to please everyone. Besides, the only opinion that truly matters is God's. When you start focusing on God's voice instead of others, you will find that you are free to be yourself, follow your convictions, and live your life to the fullest.

Try saying, "I love being myself because God created me as a unique individual, and there will never be anyone like me." (See Genesis 1:27, Psalm 139:14, Ephesians 2:10)

I can't fall in love, or I'll get my heart broken.

Love often involves taking risks and opening yourself up to vulnerability, including the possibility of heartbreak or rejection. While it may be tempting to guard your heart against pain by avoiding love altogether, by doing so, you may miss out on the joy and fulfillment love can bring. Rather than blocking yourself from love, it's important to use discernment, wisdom, and healthy boundaries when opening your heart to another.

Trusting in God's plan and purpose, even when there's a risk of heartbreak, is essential. Keep in mind that rejection can sometimes serve as a tool for character development and spiritual growth. Just as Jesus faced rejection, His love endured, even to the point of death. His ability to do so stemmed from His complete trust and love for God the Father. By following His example and cultivating an intimate relationship with Jesus, you'll gain the courage to embrace vulnerability and love others with a healed heart.

Rather, hold on to the belief that "Jesus will lead me to the person who is right for me, and I'll be able to love again with an open and healed heart." (See Psalm 32:8, Ephesians 3:17-19, 1 Corinthians 13:4-7)

I can't pursue my dreams, or I may fail.

Failure is common, even among the most successful individuals who have experienced multiple setbacks before reaching their goals. Taking risks and stepping outside your comfort zone are necessary parts of the process. If you never fail, it likely means you are not trying hard enough. To follow your dreams, you must not allow the fear of failure, the unknown, or what others may think to hold you back.

When things don't work out, what you do next is crucial. Failures can become successes if you are willing to learn from your mistakes and try again. Don't give up so easily. Victory will surely follow if you persevere and put your faith in God.

Adopt this belief instead: "I will pursue the dreams God has placed in my heart, and He will help me accomplish them." (See Deuteronomy 31:6, Proverbs 16:3, Philippians 4:13)

It's too late to pursue my dreams.

Age should never be a limiting factor in pursuing your dreams because only your beliefs can hold you back. Society may try to impose certain norms, but you should keep them from defining what you can and cannot do. Remember, anything is possible with faith, just like Abraham and Sarah, who had a child in their old age.

Even if you have made poor choices in the past and feel like you have delayed your destiny, do not lose hope. God can restore wasted time, and there is no time limit when working with Him. Colonel Sanders is a perfect example of this, having created his famous "original recipe" for Kentucky Fried Chicken at age forty-nine.[vii] Although he didn't begin franchising until he was sixty-five, he eventually sold the business at the age of seventy-four, and it is now one of the world's largest fast-food restaurant chains.

Consider the belief that "It's never too late to pursue my dreams. If I partner with God and act now, He can restore the lost time." (See Genesis 18:14, Joel 2:25, Philippians 1:6)

I don't need to be successful; therefore, I won't work toward success in achieving my dreams.

Some people think being content means they shouldn't strive for success, but that's far from the truth. God instills desires and dreams within you to enable you to achieve success. As you prosper, you can utilize your position, knowledge, experience, resources, talents, and money to help others. When you have the right motives and recognize that everything you have belongs to God, your success brings Him glory.

Replace the lie with this belief instead: "God wants me to succeed in pursuing my dreams, ensuring they align with

His purpose for my life. My success serves to glorify Him and positively impact others, reflecting His love and goodness." (See Deuteronomy 30:9, Jeremiah 29:11, 3 John 1:2)

I can't trust people because I've experienced betrayal before.

Betrayal is a negative experience that causes you to guard yourself. While this is a natural response to avoid getting hurt, it can limit you from forming meaningful relationships with others.

Experiencing betrayal never feels good, but it shouldn't lead you to isolate yourself from others. A bad experience shouldn't stop you from trusting other people. Doing so would only keep you from the great friendships and divine connections you can make.

Rather, stand on the belief that "My trust is ultimately in God; therefore, I can trust others by asking Him for wisdom and discernment in whom to trust and with what things." (See Psalm 118:8-9, Proverbs 3:5-6, James 1:5)

I can't ask for what I want because I may get rejected.

In some cases, rejection can be a form of protection from God. By rejecting your desires, He may be keeping you from a decision that could cause harm in the future. It's better to experience the pain of rejection now than to suffer greater consequences later on. For example, if you don't get the job you applied for, it could be because God has something better for you.

Say this instead, "I can ask for what I want, and if I get rejected, it could mean that the timing isn't right or because God has a better plan for me." (See Isaiah 41:9, Psalm 37:4, Romans 8:28)

I can't show anger because it's a lack of self-control.

Anger is a powerful emotion that many people avoid showing. You may struggle with this belief if you were raised in a home where you weren't allowed to express your emotions freely or if you witnessed anger displayed in a way that made you fearful.

When uncontrolled, anger can be sinful and dangerous, but it can bring forth good and righteous results when motivated by the right reasons. Jesus showed anger without sinning. Sometimes, we should be angry, especially concerning what God is angry about. Suppressing anger can lead to anxiety, depression, and social withdrawal.

Try replacing the lie with this belief: "I can express anger that may bring forth good and righteous results as long as my motives are pure, and I do not sin." (See Matthew 21:12-13, James 1:19-20, Ephesians 4:26)

Keep in mind this list is not comprehensive. Whether you identify these lies or grapple with different ones, I encourage you to turn to the Holy Spirit for guidance. Ask for His help in creating new beliefs based on the truth found in the Scriptures. Then, make a habit of meditating on them daily. Every time you embrace these godly beliefs, you dismantle a brick from the stronghold, and in time, your actions and circumstances will reflect your newfound convictions.

ACTIVATIONS

1. Take a moment to identify any ungodly beliefs you hold, along with the negative behaviors, expectations, or experiences that result from them. Write down your reflections to gain insight and clarity.

2. Ask the Holy Spirit to help you in replacing these beliefs with godly ones that are rooted in Scripture. Take note of the new beliefs and reflect on them for at least twenty-one days. Journal any changes you observe as you embrace the truth instead of the lie.

CHAPTER 7

Speaking Life-Giving Words

*"As we must account for every idle word,
so must we account for every idle silence."*
~Benjamin Franklin

WORDS THAT HEAL

Carla arrived at my house for our monthly prayer meeting with distressing news. She had just been diagnosed with oral cancer and was understandably anxious about her surgery scheduled for the next day. Following worship, we gathered around Carla to spend time interceding for her. We took turns laying hands on her, praying, and decreeing healing scriptures over her.

Sitting next to Carla, I distinctly recall feeling an overwhelming sense of God's presence. While praying, I felt compelled to command the cancer to "dissipate"— a word

I don't typically use when praying for healing. At the moment, I didn't think much of it. After each of us prayed, everyone in the room lingered in silence, immersed in the profound, weighty atmosphere of peace. The meeting stretched longer than usual. When we finally concluded, Carla left feeling uplifted and ready to face her surgery.

The following day, I received a call from Carla, her voice filled with joy and excitement. Her doctor, who had evaluated her just before the scheduled operation, was astonished by the considerable decrease in her cancerous lesions since her last appointment. The lesions had indeed dissipated, reversing their symptoms. With no further need for surgery, he canceled the procedure.

Several weeks later, at her follow-up appointment, the doctor confirmed that there were no remaining signs of cancer. Carla attributed this miraculous turn of events to divine intervention, giving all glory to God for her complete healing.

THE POWER OF WORDS

Have you ever contemplated the profound impact your words can have? Proverbs 18:21 (ESV) states, "Death and life are in the power of the tongue, and those who love it will eat its fruits." This scripture teaches that our words have significant consequences, leading to either "life" or "death" based on what we speak.

Words possess immense power, capable of blessing or cursing. The tongue can be an instrument that builds up and heals or a weapon that tears down and harms. Therefore, it's wise for us to carefully consider our words before we speak, as we will reap the fruit of our words, whether sweet or bitter.

We can shape our lives and achieve success through the words we choose. Whether those words are encouraging and uplifting or negative and critical, they will become our reality. We breathe life into the words we speak, and whether we realize it or not, we are prophesying our future.

Our conversations often reflect our spiritual health and reveal the state of our hearts. Jesus underlines this concept in Luke 6:45 (NAS), where he teaches, "The good man out of the good treasure of his heart brings forth what is good; and the evil man out of the evil treasure brings forth what is evil; for his mouth speaks from that which fills his heart." Therefore, if evil is in our hearts, it will be evident in our speech; the same goes for good.

Real change in our speech starts by addressing the underlying condition of our hearts. A wounded heart may result in harsh or judgmental words, while a healed heart is more likely to inspire and encourage. For this reason, prioritizing the healing of our hearts is essential, rather than just trying to change our words. True transformation of our speech, which leads to life-giving conversations, is only achievable when we address and resolve the deeper issues within our hearts.

James 3 illustrates the power of our words. He compares the tongue to a bit that controls a powerful horse, a rudder that directs a large ship, and a spark capable of igniting a vast forest. These examples show how something as small as a tongue can tremendously impact us, effortlessly steering us in the wrong direction. That is why we must exercise caution in the words we speak.

In its natural, sinful state, the tongue is like a small fire that spreads and causes harm to other parts of the body. If we don't control it, it can lead us down a destructive path, causing problems wherever it goes. James further cautions against the inconsistency of praising God while cursing people created in His image. This contradiction should not come out of the same mouth. As believers, we should strive to control our speech through the power of the Holy Spirit, deliberately choosing to speak words of blessing.

From the very beginning, the Bible reveals the profound power of the spoken word. Genesis 1 describes how God created the entire world by simply speaking it into existence. Hebrews 1:3 adds that Jesus, reflecting God's glory and being His exact likeness, maintains the universe with the mighty power of His spoken word.

Being made in God's image, we possess the ability to create through our words. By speaking God's Word into our circumstances, we shape the life He intended for us. This principle implies that His Word also holds the power to remove any obstacles hindering the accomplishment of God's will. Just as Jesus was fully aware of the transformative power of His words, we, too, should speak with purpose and faith.

In Mark 11, Jesus powerfully demonstrates the impact of His speech when He encounters a barren fig tree. He curses it with just a few spoken words, and the tree withers instantly. This act wasn't simply out of frustration due to its lack of fruit. In the Bible, the fig tree is often a metaphor for the nation of Israel.[viii] Therefore, Jesus' curse symbolized a deeper rebuke of Israel's spiritual barrenness, representing those who claim to follow a religious faith but have no relationship with Christ.

Another example highlighting Jesus' command over nature is found in Mark 4:35-41 (NIV), where he calms a stormy sea with His words, leaving His disciples amazed and questioning, "Who is this? Even the wind and the waves obey Him." These incidents not only emphasize the power of Jesus' words but also His authority over the physical and spiritual realms.

We are called to actively utilize the power of God's Word in our daily lives. Job 22:28 (NAS) states, "You will also decree a thing, and it will be established for you; and light will shine on your ways." In this context, "decree" means to issue an authoritative command.[ix] As God's children, decreeing His promises with faith invites His intervention.

Jeremiah 1:12 confirms that God watches over His word to perform it. This concept can be applied practically, such as when praying for healing. When someone we know suffers from pain or illness, it's not enough to pray for healing alone. Instead, we should take a proactive stance by decreeing God's Word and using the power of our words to boldly address the pain or sickness, commanding it to leave in Jesus' name. Then, with assurance, confidently declare to the person, "By His stripes, you are healed!"

RESPONDING WITH THE WORD

In Matthew 4:1-11 (NAS), Jesus demonstrated the power of the written Word of God in overcoming temptation. Satan attempted to make Jesus doubt His identity, questioning, "If you are the Son of God, command that these stones become bread." This tactic mirrors how Satan sowed doubt in the minds of Adam and Eve in the Garden of Eden.

Jesus answered, "It is written, 'Man shall not live on bread alone, but on every word that comes out of the mouth of God.'" Again, Satan tempted Jesus by taking Him to stand on the pinnacle of the temple, "If you are the Son of God, throw Yourself down." Then Satan quoted Scripture himself, "For it is written: He will give His angels orders concerning you; and on their hands they will lift you up, so that you do not strike your foot against a stone."

Aware that it's wrong to misuse His powers, Jesus countered, "On the other hand, it is written: You shall not put the Lord your God to the test." Finally, after Satan's third temptation, offering Jesus worldly power in exchange for worship, Jesus firmly commanded, "Go away, Satan! For it is written: You shall worship the Lord your God, and serve Him only." With this, Satan departed, and angels came to minister to Jesus.

Like Jesus, when we are in a spiritual battle, we resist Satan with Scripture. Hebrews 4:12 (NLT) says, "For the Word of God is alive and powerful. It is sharper than the sharpest two-edged sword, cutting between soul and spirit, between joint and marrow. It exposes our innermost thoughts and desires." Just as a soldier defeats an enemy with a sword, we can similarly wield God's Word to cut through and conquer the temptations of Satan in our spiritual warfare.

WATCH YOUR WORDS

Jesus is very clear about the importance of our speech, as He explains in Matthew 12:36-37 (NKJV), "But I say to you that for every idle word men may speak, they will give account of it in the day of judgment. For by your words you will be justified, and by your words you will be condemned." Speaking idle or careless words without careful consideration is useless for productive communication.

We should reflect on the phrases or expressions we use thoughtlessly, often influenced by our upbringing or environment. If we pay close attention, we might notice that we often speak words we don't truly mean. Sayings like, "You're killing me," "I'm so stupid," and "That drives me crazy" are examples of such idle words.

Sometimes, the small, unguarded comments that slip out can reveal much about our character. Jesus emphasizes this in Matthew 12:36, warning that every empty, careless word spoken will be held accountable, as they often unveil our inner thoughts and beliefs.

Ultimately, we speak what we believe, and the words spoken from our mouths will shape our lives and impact others around us. Rather than using meaningless words, let's be intentional with our speech, aligning our words with God's purposes. Ephesians 4:29 (NIV) advises, "Do not let any unwholesome talk come out of your mouths, but only what is helpful for building others up according to their needs, that it may benefit those who listen."

In a world where words are frequently used to curse and bring others down, we, as followers of Christ, are called to a higher standard. God has entrusted us with the creative power to transform our environment through speaking blessings and life-giving words. Through the spoken Word of God, infused with love, power, and grace, we conquer worldly temptations, shape our lives, and illuminate our world with His hope and light.

ACTIVATIONS

1. How can you harness the power of your words to both constructively build and wisely dismantle to bring about God's will in your life and surroundings?

2. Reflect on any habitual phrases or "idle words" you commonly use. What situations typically prompt you to say these words? Contemplate whether they truly reflect your intentions and beliefs. When you feel tempted to use these phrases, what life-giving words can you replace them with?

3. Consider someone in need of a miracle, whether it's for yourself or another individual. How can you pray most effectively, and which specific scriptures could you confidently use to support the desired miracle?

CHAPTER 8

Walking in Wholeness

"Our bodies are our gardens
to which our wills are gardeners."
-William Shakespeare

SLIPPING TO THE BOTTOM OF THE LIST

I felt like a volcano ready to erupt, with pressure mounting from all directions. Years of frustration led me to despair, and I couldn't understand how I had reached that point. Initially, as a newlywed, I was happy as can be. However, as the years passed, I faced numerous challenges seemingly all at once. Juggling responsibilities in my family life, work, and ministry became overwhelming. Self-care, once a priority, now only happened when I had extra time and money to spare.

Becoming a busy mother of three, including twins, happened quickly for me. My husband and I worked opposite schedules, leaving hardly any time for family together, let alone date nights. On top of that, we faced financial struggles due to a bad investment. The pressure continued to build as my supervisor at work began compiling information in an attempt to fire me. We had no choice but to cancel the one thing we looked forward to as a family—our yearly vacation.

On the brink of burnout, I struggled to keep up with the women's ministry I was leading. I used my requested vacation days to rest and catch up on long-neglected tasks. Among these was my yearly wellness check-up, which I assumed would be quick and easy; however, things unfolded differently than expected.

THE WAKE-UP CALL

A few days later, my doctor informed me that my mammogram results had returned positive for breast cancer. The news came as a shock since my mother had the same diagnosis just a year before. In hindsight, canceling our vacation was a blessing in disguise. If we hadn't called it off, I might have delayed my check-up another year or more, potentially leading to a more severe outcome.

Thankfully, because I went when I did, the cancer was caught at an early stage.

The diagnosis brought my hectic life to an abrupt halt and marked the beginning of my journey toward healing and wholeness. As I reflected on the possible contributors to my condition, I realized that chronic stress, coupled with a genetic predisposition, may have played a significant role. This sudden realization served as a profound wake-up call, prompting me to make considerable changes in my life.

I came to realize I had been measuring my self-worth based on how much I did for others, often neglecting my own needs in the process. Through this understanding, I learned the critical importance of self-care. Making my health and well-being a priority involved recognizing my inherent value as a child of God and responsibly caring for my body, the temple of the Holy Spirit.

While attending to my health, I passed the leadership of the women's ministry to someone else. My focus shifted from serving in that capacity to nurturing my relationship with God. Each day began in God's presence, where I sought guidance from the Holy Spirit through worship and the Word. This sacred space allowed me to be led from a place of rest. Additionally, I made improvements to my diet and exercise habits, and I prioritized quality time with my family.

As a result, I transitioned from a state of depletion and anxiety to one of peace and contentment. I found comfort in the certainty of my identity secured in God, no longer needing validation from others.

SPIRIT, SOUL, AND BODY

The triune nature of God—Father, Son, and Holy Spirit—is reflected in humans, who are created in His image. Similarly, we are triune beings composed of spirit, soul, and body. The health of each of these parts is intricately linked; when one suffers, it can negatively affect the others. This interconnectedness forms the complete tapestry of our being. Therefore, achieving and maintaining wholeness requires nurturing all three components, which God intends to function together in harmony for an optimal life.

The Apostle Paul affirms the importance of a holistic approach to our being in 1 Thessalonians 5:23 (KJV). In his letter to the church, he writes, "And the very God of peace sanctify you wholly; and I pray God your whole spirit and soul and body be preserved blameless unto the coming of our Lord Jesus Christ." By mentioning the spirit first, Paul emphasizes our primary identity as spiritual beings guided by the Holy Spirit. This perspective contrasts the modern world's fixation on the physical body, often at the expense of the soul and spirit.

For example, consider a person dealing with the emotional pain of rejection who focuses solely on their physical health, engaging in excessive exercise to feel more accepted. Despite their efforts to improve their outward appearance, the underlying feelings of rejection may continue to linger if they remain unaddressed.

Paul's teachings indicate that sanctification should be "through and through," signifying a comprehensive process. It encompasses not only external aspects but places greater emphasis on inner transformation. This perspective is echoed in 1 Timothy 4:8 (NLT), which states, "Physical training is good, but training for godliness is much better, promising benefits in this life and in the life to come."

A PLACE OF WHOLENESS

As believers, we are called to serve others in obedience to Christ. Yet, we shouldn't neglect our own needs in the process, as doing so can lead to burnout and frustration. While serving is a core principle of our faith, our motivation should not be self-seeking or for the sake of gaining approval; such motives are not aligned with God's will and often point to a need for emotional healing.

In the process of serving others, it's important to remember that our lives serve a higher purpose beyond personal fulfillment; they are dedicated to serving God and answering His call for us. Protecting this calling requires both spiritual and emotional health, enabling us to forgive and love others as commanded by God, while also maintaining physical health to sustain our service. Therefore, tending to our overall well-being is essential for accomplishing the tasks and purposes God has ordained for us.

Prioritizing our well-being is not selfish; instead, it's recognizing that neglecting self-care can hinder our ability to help others effectively. Consider the safety instructions on an airplane: passengers are advised to secure their own oxygen masks before assisting others. This principle highlights a vital truth—if we're struggling, our ability to support those relying on us is compromised. By dedicating time to self-care, we become better equipped to assist those around us.

In 1 Corinthians 3:16-17, Paul imparts a profound truth that we all should consider: our bodies are more than flesh and bone, they are sacred temples that house God's spirit, and he cautions against causing them any harm. This message is reinforced in 1 Corinthians 6:19-20, where Paul reminds us that our bodies are entrusted to us by God, sanctified by His Spirit, and thus, not solely our own. Having been bought at a price, each of us holds a personal responsibility to honor God in caring for our bodies.

Honoring this temple goes beyond just maintaining a healthy lifestyle and self-respect; it also encompasses the inner work of emotional and spiritual healing. Integral to this healing are practices like forgiveness and repentance, which are explored in greater depth in "Healing Your Heart," the second book in the Destined to Shine series.

Ultimately, it is our duty to nurture every facet of our being—spirit, soul, and body. Embracing wholeness empowers us to live with purity and vitality, enabling us to serve others, glorify God, and fully experience the abundant life He has promised.

SELF-CARE IN LEADERSHIP

Leading from a place of wholeness significantly impacts our effectiveness. We often face the challenge of balancing busy schedules and the responsibility of caring for others, which can quickly push self-care to the background. Whether we are parents, ministers, or business owners, we must recognize that neglecting our well-being can have visible consequences, especially during testing times. What's happening inside us often manifests externally, particularly when issues arise that can lead to loss of control, affecting every aspect of our lives.

During times of stress, it becomes even more critical for us to be intentional about self-care. Numerous studies have shown that stress is a significant contributor to illnesses. Therefore, taking time to rest and recharge isn't just beneficial—it's necessary for maintaining good health. The creation story in Genesis reminds us that even God rested on the seventh day, demonstrating the need for rest. We find restoration and peace for our souls when we stop striving and rest in His presence.

Jesus speaks to this in Matthew 11:28-30 (TM): "Are you tired? Worn out? Burned out on religion? Come to me. Get away with me and you'll recover your life. I'll show you how to take a real rest. Walk with me and work with me—watch how I do it. Learn the unforced rhythms of grace. I won't lay anything heavy or ill-fitting on you. Keep company with me and you'll learn to live freely and lightly."

As leaders, we must remember that we are constantly under the watchful eye of others, who notice our appearance, behavior, and words. This is particularly true for parents, who have a significant role in setting an example. Children observe and absorb every aspect of our lives. Therefore, we should reflect on whether our daily habits are ones we would want them to model. Upholding high standards in disciplines such as rising early, spending time with God, keeping our environments clean, eating healthy meals, working diligently, and maintaining an exercise routine sets a powerful example.

These standards not only impact those around us but also contribute to our personal growth. Leading by example paves the way for others to follow, thereby earning their respect and gratitude.

As we journey forward, prioritizing self-care and exemplifying strong leadership, it's important to recognize the unique roles each of us plays. Reflect on your own practices and leadership style. Consider if you are living as the best version of yourself for God, your family, employees, clients, and friends.

Take a moment to evaluate your daily routines and ask yourself if they are the kind you'd want others to emulate.

Remember, your personal development not only benefits yourself but also sets a strong example for those around you.

Maintaining a balanced self-care routine is key to your overall well-being. Keep in mind that effective self-care is highly personalized; the practices that work for one person may not suit another. It's essential to find a self-care routine that works with your needs. To avoid feeling overwhelmed, consider introducing one new self-care practice at a time, gradually introducing it into your routine until it becomes a consistent habit.

To support you in achieving a balanced approach to self-care, here is a list of suggestions:

- **Commune with God**—Begin each day by intimately connecting with the Lord through reading his Word, prayer, and worship. This personal time in communion invites peace and clarity into your day, guided by God's wisdom.

- **Keep a journal**—Maintain separate journals to document your daily gratitude, dreams, conversations with God, notes, and personal goals. Use this personal space for reflection to appreciate

God's work in your life and align with His goals and purposes.

- **Get adequate rest**—View rest as a gift from God that rejuvenates your body and mind. Getting enough sleep is vital to avoid burnout, as it leads to improved energy and productivity. Consider setting a bedtime alarm to commit to this practice.

- **Eat healthy**—Choose to nourish your body with wholesome foods, treating it as the temple of God. Healthy eating sustains energy and vitality, aligning with God's design for your well-being.

- **Exercise regularly**—Honor your body by stewarding it well through regular exercise. It not only boosts physical health but also releases endorphins, a natural antidepressant, promoting mental and emotional well-being.

- **Spend time in nature**—Embrace God's creation by walking or running outdoors. This personal interaction with nature not only refreshes your spirit but also enhances your connection with God and boosts creativity.

- **Go on spiritual retreats**—Dedicate time for retreats to seek God's presence, away from daily responsibilities. Whether in solitude or with fellow believers, retreats can rejuvenate your spirit and deepen your connection with Him.

- **Keep a clean environment**—Maintain cleanliness and organize your surroundings as it facilitates greater focus. A tidy environment enhances mental clarity and emotional peace, aligning with God's call for orderliness.

- **Detox from social media**—Periodically disconnect from the noise and distractions of the digital world to find God's peace and presence. This personal discipline helps maintain focus on what truly matters.

- **Seek expert advice**—Don't hesitate to consult with a mentor, counselor, or coach when facing challenges or feeling stuck. Seeking guidance is a step toward healing and growth, helping you move forward with success.

- **Spend time with friends**— Sitting with a friend over a cup of coffee or a meal can emotionally charge and fill you. It's an opportunity for fellowship and building relationships.

- **Enjoy laughter**—Incorporate laughter into your daily routine as it is good medicine. Watching a comedy or enjoying funny moments can cheer you up and provide daily relief from stress.

- **Continue to learn**—Invest in your personal and spiritual growth through books, courses, or workshops. Learning from others not only boosts motivation and accountability but also helps you save time.

- **Plan an exciting trip**—Anticipating a trip can motivate you to work diligently. Traveling is an opportunity to refresh and explore God's creation in diverse places.

- **Find a hobby**—Explore creative hobbies such as painting, photography, or playing an instrument. These activities allow you to express your God-given talents and discover joy in creativity.

Caring for your physical, emotional, and spiritual needs is a necessary step toward living authentically and in alignment with your true identity. It's important to recognize that self-care must have a foundation in God, as He is deeply concerned for your overall well-being.

Responsible stewardship of your life honors God and acknowledges His role in guiding your leadership.

Practicing self-care opens the door to heightened peace, greater confidence, and improved health, equipping you to lead effectively and care for others. Walking in wholeness, as a child of God, is a pathway to success in fulfilling your purpose and radiating His love to those around you.

ACTIVATIONS

1. On a scale of one to ten, how would you rate your level of self-care? Can you identify specific goals to enhance your self-care routine?

2. Choose one new self-care habit you plan to integrate into your life this week. What steps will you take to ensure its implementation?

About the Author

Mary Chalhoub is a prophetic voice, worshiper, and speaker who is passionate about helping believers live the authentic, victorious life God has designed for them. Drawing sons and daughters to the heart of the Father, she carries a revival anointing that inspires them to rise and respond to God's call. Having ministered in over ten countries, Mary holds a global vision for awakening and transformation.

She founded Kingdom Roar, a dynamic network that equips and supports prophetic creatives and leaders through training and collaboration. Dedicated to a thriving community, Mary brings together like-minded individuals who seek to deepen their intimacy with God and discern His voice, all while activating and strengthening their prophetic callings. The mentorship, courses, and personalized coaching, available online and in-person, empower participants to find their unique voices, thereby unlocking their potential for lasting kingdom impact. For more information, visit www.kingdomroar.co.

Mary resides with her husband and three children in Houston, Texas. In her free time, she enjoys quality time with her family, writing music, painting, and playing with her dogs—who are basically her family, too! Learn more at www.marychalhoub.com.

Connect with Mary:

Facebook: www.FB.com/marychalhoubpage

Instagram: www.instagram.com/marychalhoub

YouTube: www.YouTube.com/@marychalhoub

To book Mary Chalhoub for your next event:
www.marychalhoub.com/invite

More Resources from Mary Chalhoub

If you've found value in reading this book and want to continue your transformation journey, visit www.marychalhoub.com for more resources.

Explore additional books in the series, sign up for courses, and take advantage of one-on-one coaching sessions with Mary Chalhoub to accelerate your growth.

Start living your God-given dreams with joy, confidence, and purpose today!

Endnotes

[i] Adamas: Meaning, Translation - Wordsense. https://www.wordsense.eu/Adamas/.

[ii] Hinkle, A.C. (2021) Metamorfoo, Practical Theology Today. Available at: https://practicaltheologytoday.com/2019/03/26/metamorfoo/

[iii] "Confidence (n.)." Etymology, https://www.etymonline.com/word/Confidence.

[iv] "Esteem (v.)." Etymology, https://www.etymonline.com/word/esteem.

[v] "Stronghold." Merriam-Webster.com Dictionary, Merriam-Webster, https://www.merriam-webster.com/dictionary/stronghold.

[vi] Maltz, Maxwell. Psycho-Cybernetics. Simon & Schuster, 1960. ISBN 978-0671700751

[vii] Colonel Sanders (2024) Wikipedia. Available at: https://en.wikipedia.org/wiki/Colonel_Sanders.

[viii] Mark 11:13 BibleRef.com. Available at: https://www.bibleref.com/Mark/11/Mark-11-13.html

[ix] Decree definition & meaning Merriam-Webster. Available at: https://www.merriam-webster.com/dictionary/decree.